Cokesbury's
GALACTIC BLAST

A Cosmic Adventure Praising God!

Asse... r

MW00964980

Contents

A Cosmic Adventure Praising God!

Day	Bible Story	Praise Phrase	Bible Booster	Discovery Time
Session 1 Mission: Creation of the Universe	**Genesis 1:1–2:4** Space Connection: **Earth**	**Our God is wonderful! Praise God!** Color of the day: **Green**	The earth is the Lord's and all that is in it, the world, and those who live in it. (Psalm 24:1, NRSV)	★ And Then There Was Light ★ Perfect Motion ★ Gravity Grabs
Session 2 Mission: Elijah at Mt. Horeb	**1 Kings 19:4-18** Space Connection: **Moon**	**Our God is incredible! Praise God!** Color of the day: **Red**	But for me it is good to be near God. (Psalm 73:28a, NRSV)	★ Listening ★ Seeing and Knowing
Session 3 Mission: The Woman at the Well	**John 4:1-42** Space Connection: **Stars**	**Our God is amazing! Praise God!** Color of the day: **Blue**	O Lord, you have searched me and known me. (Psalm 139:1, NRSV)	★ Daytime Starlight ★ Nighttime Starlight ★ Twinkling Stars
Session 4 Mission: A Blind Beggar in Jericho	**Luke 18:35-43** Space Connection: **Comet**	**Our God is magnificent! Praise God!** Color of the day: **Yellow**	The voice of the Lord is powerful; the voice of the Lord is full of majesty. (Psalm 29:4, NRSV)	★ Beggar Is Not a Pushover ★ What Do You See?
Session 5 Mission: Two Disciples in Emmaus	**Luke 24:13-32** Space Connection: **Supernova**	**Our God is awesome! Praise God!** Color of the day: **Purple**	The Lord lives! Praise be to my Rock! Exalted be God my Savior! (Psalm 18:46, NIV)	★ Light Tag ★ Excitement Explosion

Snack	Mission	Crafts	Recreation	Music
★ **Galactic Praise Snackers** **Easy Snacks** ★ String Cheese Shuttles ★ Cosmic Candy **Healthy Snack** ★ Fruit Cocktail Fuel	**Katie's Garden** (Katie Stagliano)	★ Galactic Sand Art (all ages) ★ Creation Wall Hanging & Quilt (elementary/tween) ★ Planet Earth Tissue Creation (preschool)	★ Creation Station Relay ★ Planet Toss ★ Guess God's Wonders	★ "Galactic Blast" ★ "Praise God" ★ "It's Wonderful"
★ **Near Me Moon Cakes** **Easy Snacks** ★ Over-the-Moon Pies ★ Moonbeam Muffins **Healthy Snack** ★ Lunar Bagels	**Ashlee's Toy Closet** (Ashlee Smith)	★ Moonbeam Tambourine (all ages) ★ Praise God Canvas Art (all ages)	★ Stick to It! ★ Whisper on the Mountain ★ Hear Me, Elijah!	★ "You and Me Together" ★ "Revolution" ★ "Fill Me With Praises"
★ **Amazing Space Mix** **Easy Snacks** ★ Amazing Space Mix II ★ Jacob's Well Dips **Healthy Snack** ★ Constellation Club Sandwiches	**Maxwell's Birthday Wish** (Maxwell Lawson)	★ Spectacular Star Clappers (all ages) ★ Constellation Magnets (elementary/tween) ★ Sparkling Stars (preschool)	★ Star Snatch ★ Living Water Fill-Up ★ Memory Booster	★ "A-M-A-Z-I-N-G" ★ "A New Life in Me"
★ **Comet Coolers** **Easy Snacks** ★ Jericho Juicers ★ Magnificent Praise Pops **Healthy Snack** ★ Starship Smoothie	**A Nickelby Difference** (Nicholas Marriam and Shelby McKnew)	★ God Cares Comet Frame (all ages) ★ Cosmic Craft Photo Frame (all ages) ★ Cosmic Craft Memory Page (all ages)	★ See Again! ★ Melt the Comet ★ Who Is It?	★ "God of Wonders" ★ "Let Everything That Has Breath"
★ **Supernova Sundaes** **Easy Snacks** ★ Intergalactic Ice Cream Cups ★ Space Cadet Ice Cream **Healthy Snack** ★ Go Galactic Yogurt	**Kennedy Cares** (Kennedy Jet Kulish)	★ Praise Supernova (all ages) ★ Solar Bead Cross Necklace (elementary/tween) ★ Cosmic Craft Stencils (preschool)	★ Awesome Stepping ★ Supernova Explosion ★ Old To New	★ Sing your favorites!

Assembly Time

Before your cadets "spacewalk" to their activity centers, begin each cosmic adventure by gathering together on the starship Galactic Praise.

The Commander, Galileo, and the VBS GPS

Aboard the starship Galactic Praise, the cadets meet the starship's commander and the commander's assistant, Galileo the Gorilla. While the commander prepares the cadets for each session's mission, Galileo's fun-loving spirit and inquisitive nature add humor and a childlike perspective. Galileo also explains the significance of his green fur and the importance of being "green" every day. (See "The Green Connection.")

The commander and Galileo receive assistance from the VBS GPS (Galactic Praise Satellite), which offers a preview of and insight into each mission. (The VBS GPS footage is found on the *Adventure Video for Assembly Time DVD*.) Once awakened by the daily Praise Phrase, the VBS GPS presents the cadets with fun facts and stunning visuals about various outer space phenomena. In addition, the VBS GPS gives cadets a peek at where the Bible stories take place.

The "Green" Connection

Once Galileo discovers the excitement of being "green," he's eager to share his eco-friendly lifestyle with your cadets by offering them a different "green" challenge for each session to be completed before they return. Taken together, these "green" tips empower your cadets to care for the wonderful creation God has made for them.

★ **Session One:** Galileo asks the cadets to conserve energy by turning off lights, toys, or other electronics when they aren't in use.

★ **Session Two:** Galileo suggests the cadets find new uses for toys and clothing they have outgrown.

★ **Session Three:** Galileo reminds the cadets to conserve water.

★ **Session Four:** Galileo advises the cadets to keep God's Earth beautiful by putting litter and trash where they belong.

★ **Session Five:** Galileo recommends that your cadets recycle whenever they have the opportunity.

Adventure Video for Assembly Time DVD/CD-ROM

This resource features video segments for the VBS GPS, complete with the GPS voiceover and actual footage from outer space and from the Bible mission locations. The DVD also contains sign language demonstrations for the Bible Booster memory verses. The CD-ROM has recorded Galileo puppet dialogue and PDF versions of all assembly scripts.

To play the VBS GPS segments, put the DVD in the DVD tray. Press "play" and wait for the selection menu screen. Use the arrow keys on the DVD remote to highlight the selection to play. When your choice is selected, press "enter/play." The screen will be black. Press "enter/play" again to begin the selection. See the back cover of the *Adventure Video DVD* jacket for video segment lengths.

To use the CD-ROM for Galieo's dialogue, follow the *Assembly Leader*. Press "play" each time Galileo has a line; press "pause" after each line.

The Praise Phrase

During each assembly, the commander and Galileo introduce the session's Praise Phrase as they "wake up" the VBS GPS. This call-and-response phrase is then used throughout the day to keep the children connected to GALACTIC BLAST's emphasis on praising God. Each Praise Phrase has two parts: a statement about God, followed by a "Praise God!" response.

★ **Session One:** Our God is wonderful! Praise God!
★ **Session Two:** Our God is incredible! Praise God!
★ **Session Three:** Our God is amazing! Praise God!
★ **Session Four:** Our God is magnificent! Praise God!
★ **Session Five:** Our God is awesome! Praise God!

Closing Celebration Scripts

In addition to complete scripts for every opening and closing assembly, this resource also provides a script for a closing celebration. This celebration can be an evening performance after VBS is over or a Sunday morning assembly.

You will also find traditional and contemporary worship service outlines if you choose to make your final celebration part of a Sunday morning worship service.

Music During Assemblies

Assembly time opens with music from the GALACTIC BLAST program. The recommended songs for each assembly, closing celebration, and worship service are listed below.

Session One Opening
★ "Galactic Blast"
★ "Praise God"

Session One Closing
★ "It's Wonderful"
★ "Praise God"

Session Two Opening
★ "Galactic Blast"
★ "It's Wonderful"

Session Two Closing
★ "You and Me Together"
★ "Revolution"

Session Three Opening
★ "Revolution"
★ "Praise God"

Session Three Closing
★ "A-M-A-Z-I-N-G"
★ "A New Life in Me"
★ "Fill Me With Praises"

Session Four Opening
★ "It's Wonderful"
★ "You and Me Together"

Session Four Closing
★ "You and Me Together"
★ "God of Wonders"

Session Five Opening
★ "Let Everything That Has Breath"
★ "A-M-A-Z-I-N-G"

Session Five Closing
★ "Praise God"
★ "Galactic Blast"
★ "Fill Me With Praises"

Closing Celebration
★ "Galactic Blast"
★ "Praise God"
★ "It's Wonderful"
★ "Revolution"
★ "God of Wonders"
★ "Fill Me With Praises"
★ "You and Me Together"
★ "A-M-A-Z-I-N-G"
★ "A New Life in Me"
★ "Let Everything That Has Breath"

Traditional Worship Service
★ "God of Wonders"
★ "You and Me Together"
★ "It's Wonderful"
★ "Praise God"
★ "A-M-A-Z-I-N-G"
★ "A New Life in Me"
★ "Let Everything That Has Breath"

Contemporary Worship Service
★ "God of Wonders"
★ "Let Everything That Has Breath"
★ "Revolution"
★ "A New Life in Me"
★ "It's Wonderful"

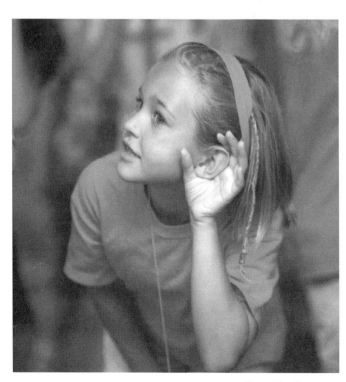

Photo: Matt Huesmann

Decorating the Starship Galactic Praise

Resources

- ☆ *Activity Center Sign,* "Starship Galactic Praise"
- ☆ *Decorating Mural*
- ☆ *Decorating Transparencies,* "Starship Galactic Praise," "Space Items I," "Space Items II"
- ☆ *Reflective Space Blankets*
- ☆ *Complete Music CD*
- ☆ *Music Video DVD*
- ☆ *Assembly Leader*
- ☆ *Adventure Video for Assembly Time DVD/CD-ROM*
- ☆ *Galileo the Gorilla Puppet*

Materials

- ☆ white or gray butcher paper
- ☆ acrylic paint
- ☆ dryer vent hoses
- ☆ laptop computer (for VBS GPS)
- ☆ tall cardboard box
- ☆ aluminum foil
- ☆ cardboard sheets
- ☆ old computer keyboards and monitors
- ☆ video game seats
- ☆ rectangular paint palettes
- ☆ plastic takeout containers
- ☆ roofing nails or pushpins
- ☆ buttons
- ☆ sturdy paper plates
- ☆ aluminum pie plates
- ☆ old CDs
- ☆ CD player
- ☆ TV or projection screen and DVD player

Additional Props

All Sessions
- ☆ astronaut jumpsuit or *Leader T-shirt* and scrub pants (for the commander)

Session One
- ☆ energy-efficient light bulb

Session Four
- ☆ painted picture of a star
- ☆ messy painted picture with clumps of glue and lots of glitter; could resemble a star
- ☆ extra glitter on Galileo

Session Five
- ☆ *Reflective Space Blanket*
- ☆ *Outreach Seed Cards* (one per child)

Decorating Tips

- ★ Hang the three panels of the *Decorating Mural* as the backdrop for your assembly. Alternately, create your own mural by using the "Space Items I" and "Space Items II" *Decorating Transparencies* to add space objects to sheets of butcher paper.

- ★ Use the "Starship Galactic Praise" *Decorating Transparency* to create window frames that go along the top and bottom edges of the mural. These frames will give the impression that you are looking through the window of the starship out at outer space. The transparency also has diagonal lines you can use to separate the large window into smaller triangular panes. We suggest constructing the frames on white or gray butcher paper.

- ★ Frame the left and right sides of the backdrop with dryer vent hoses.

- ★ Construct computer consoles in front of the backdrop. See "Creating Consoles" for detailed instructions. If you need to add width to your set, you can add additional consoles perpendicular to the mural backdrop.

- ★ Photocopy the "VBS GPS" logo from the inside back cover and affix to the lid of a laptop computer; set on top of a podium created from a box covered in aluminum foil. Set up the TV or projector and DVD player.

- ★ Create a spot for the Galileo puppeteer behind one of the computer consoles. Experiment with what works best for your set.

- ★ Cover both sides of the doors to your assembly area with *Reflective Space Blankets.* Make signs reading "CAUTION: AIRLOCK" over the doors.

- ★ Looking for other ideas for decorating your assembly area? We've included photos throughout this guide of how both larger and smaller test churches interpreted the starship concept. Because the starship Galactic Praise exists only in our imagination, you can exercise your creativity and decorate with whatever resources you have available.

Creating Consoles

This is an easy, fun, and "green" way to add detail to your starship Galactic Praise set.

1. Ask your congregation for old computer monitors and keyboards.

2. Place tables covered in floor-length table drapings in front of the assembly backdrop. Put the monitors and keyboards on these tables.

3. Use cardboard sheets painted gray or silver to ensconce the monitors and keyboards into a single console.

4. Now the fun part: Raid your supply cabinet and recycling containers to look for items to simulate the computer controls: rectangular paint palettes, plastic takeout containers, roofing nails or pushpins, buttons, sturdy paper plates, aluminum pie plates, and old CDs are some of the items we saw used. You might want to treat some items to a coat of paint, or label others with words like "ABORT" or "OXYGEN LEVEL." See the photo for ideas.

5. Elevate video game seats on a box covered in aluminum foil to complete the look. (Don't let anyone sit on the seat if the box is cardboard!)

Photo: Matt Huesmann

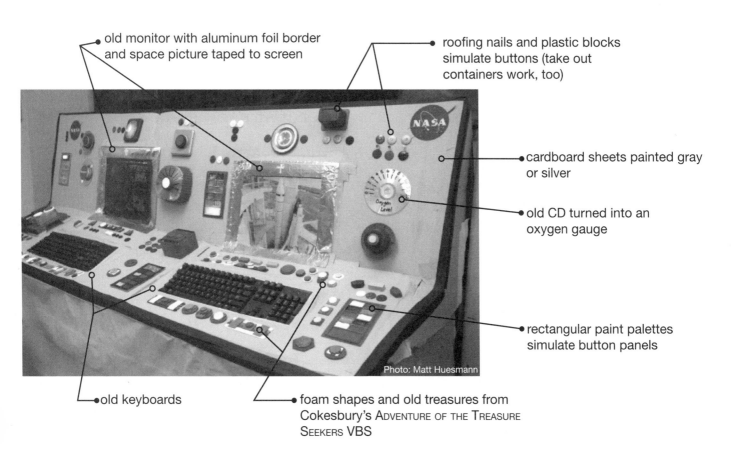

old monitor with aluminum foil border and space picture taped to screen

roofing nails and plastic blocks simulate buttons (take out containers work, too)

cardboard sheets painted gray or silver

old CD turned into an oxygen gauge

rectangular paint palettes simulate button panels

old keyboards

foam shapes and old treasures from Cokesbury's Adventure of the Treasure Seekers VBS

Photo: Matt Huesmann

Session One Opening

(The music leader teaches the children "Galactic Blast" and "Praise God." Make announcements before the skit begins.)

COMMANDER: **Hello, cadets, and welcome to the starship Galactic Praise! Are you ready for an adventure miles above the surface of the earth? I'm Commander** *(name)*. **It's my job to make sure we complete our mission: to praise our wonderful, incredible, amazing, magnificent, and awesome God!**

We're going to have an exciting time, cadets. You're going to learn about outer space, experience God's love, and meet new friends. In fact, let me introduce you to another member of our crew. Joining you in your mission to learn about outer space and the work of our Creator will be the latest in long line of animal astronauts—Galileo the Gorilla.

Now, gorillas are very shy creatures, so we have to make our new friend feel welcome. Can someone tell me what a gorilla sounds like? *(Pick someone to make gorilla noises.)* **That's great. Can everyone do that? Let's all make our gorilla noises and call Galileo.**

(Everyone makes gorilla sounds.)

GALILEO: *(Springs in very quickly)* **Who's there?** *(Sees the children and reacts as if frightened)* **Aaagh!** *(Recovers)* **Wow! You gave me a fright! I was told I was going to be the only gorilla on board.**

COMMANDER: **You are, Galileo. The cadets just wanted to make you feel welcome. But I have to ask: How did you turn green?**

GALILEO: *(Notices the color for the first time)* **What? Oh, no!** *Green?* **It must have been the accident in the cafeteria!**

COMMANDER: **There was an accident in the cafeteria?**

GALILEO: **Huh? Who said anything about an accident in the cafeteria?** *(To the children)* **Did** *you* **say anything about an accident in the cafeteria?**

COMMANDER: *(Suspicious)* **What happened?**

GALILEO: **I was looking around for a good place to build a nest. We gorillas like a comfy bed of leaves and grass to sleep on. Anyway, I thought it made sense to sleep near the food, so I went to the cafeteria. As I was looking around for some leaves and grass—you know there aren't a lot of leaves and grass on this starship?**

COMMANDER: **What happened?**

GALILEO: **I . . . well . . . you know that button on the wall in there?**

COMMANDER: **What button?**

GALILEO: **The big, red, shiny, candy-like button?**

COMMANDER: **The one that says "Do Not Push?"**

GALILEO: **Is that what it says? I'm not much of a reader. I know a little sign language, mostly the words for food, banana, ice cream—**

COMMANDER: **What happened?**

GALILEO: **—mommy, kitten, bubble gum—**

COMMANDER: **Galileo!** *What happened?*

GALILEO: **When?**

COMMANDER: **When you saw the button.**

GALILEO: **What button?**

COMMANDER: **The big red button.**

GALILEO: **The one that says "Do Not Push?"**

COMMANDER: **That's right.**

GALILEO: **I pushed it.**

COMMANDER: **Oh, no! That button controls the gravity in the cafeteria!**

GALILEO: **Is that what it does? The next thing I knew, I was floating around the room through clouds of food. There was guacamole, lime Jell-o, key lime pie—**

COMMANDER: **Oh no!**

GALILEO: **—green Kool-Aid, broccoli, bell peppers, green beans, olives—**

COMMANDER: **Galileo!**

GALILEO: **Yes, commander?**

COMMANDER: **What did you do?**

GALILEO: **I floated around in it for a while, then cleaned it up. Gorillas are very clean creatures.**

COMMANDER: **Well. . . good.**

GALILEO: **So the cafeteria is all clean!**

COMMANDER: **Great. But it looks like you're wearing a lot of it. We'll have to see about cleaning you up after the mission.**

GALILEO: **And I still need a place for my nest!**

COMMANDER: **Well, Galileo, it sounds like you've had a very busy first day, and we're just getting started. Today we're going to learn about how God created the earth.**

GALILEO: **That's exciting! I'm excited!** (To the children) **Are you excited?** (Yelling) **I'm excited!**

COMMANDER: **OK, calm down, Galileo. Cadets, Galileo** should **be excited because how God created the earth is an exciting story.**

Think about it for a second. Do you know why we call God the Creator? (Wait for responses.) **That's right! God made the entire universe. Imagine that, cadets. Before there were animals and plants, before there were mountains and oceans, before there were stars and planets, there was God.**

Let me ask you, cadets. What is the biggest thing you've ever made?

GALILEO: **That's easy! The mess in the cafeteria.**

COMMANDER: **OK, what was the biggest thing you've ever made** on purpose? **Some of you might have helped plant a garden or build a fence. Those are both big things. When we sing together, we make a big beautiful sound, don't we? But if we each took the biggest thing we ever made and put them together, it would still be smaller than the universe, right? God made the entire universe, and the Bible tells us that of all the things God created, it is Earth that makes God most proud.**

Now, what have you made that makes you the proudest?

GALILEO: **I'm going with the mess in the cafeteria again.**

COMMANDER: **That must have been some mess!**

GALILEO: **Not any more. When the gravity stopped working, I made sure all that food floated out of the cafeteria and into your quarters. Once I got everything inside, I closed the door and heard this big** sploosh.

COMMANDER: **In my** bedroom? **I'm not sure why you're proud of that, Galileo.**

GALILEO: **Creative problem solving. That's why I'm on this mission. I was the smartest gorilla at astronaut school!**

COMMANDER: **I'm sure you were. Later, we'll see if you can't come up with a creative way to clean up my bedroom.**

But right now I believe it's time for our mission briefing. For that, we'll need to consult the Vacation Bible School Galactic Praise System. Cadets, we are

lucky to have the VBS GPS. It represents the very latest in galactic praise technology.

(The screen reveals a visual sound wave. It is barely moving as snoring can be heard.)

It looks like we'll need to wake it up. To do that, we all need to yell the Praise Phrase for the day. OK?

GALILEO: I got here late, commander. I don't know what the Praise Phrase is.

COMMANDER: That's because I haven't told everyone yet. So here is how it works. Each day, I'll give you a Praise Phrase that we'll use to wake up the VBS GPS. Today's Praise Phrase is "Our God is wonderful! Praise God!" Got it?

GALILEO: Our God is wonderful! Praise God!

COMMANDER: So, if you hear someone say "Our God is wonderful!" you say "Praise God!" Right? Let's try it now. Everyone on this side of the room will say "Our God is wonderful!" And everyone on the other side will say "Praise God!" Got it?

GALILEO: I've got it, commander. My side is going to be *way* louder than your side.

COMMANDER: We'll see about that! Here we go. *(With children)* Our God is wonderful!

GALILEO: *(With children)* Praise God!

COMMANDER: That's it! Great job. Now, let's use our Praise Phrase to wake up the VBS GPS. Everyone ready? *(With children)* Our God is wonderful!

GALILEO: *(With children)* Praise God!

***************BEGIN VIDEO SEGMENT**************

COMPUTER: *(Springing to life)* Shngnhg . . . huh?! What? Oh! Hello, commander! The VBS GPS is ready with your mission briefing on the creation of the universe. We'll be focusing on your home planet, Earth.

Let's see . . . Earth . . . Earth . . . There it is! Earth is the third planet from the sun.

The Earth is over 24,901 miles around its widest point. We call this the equator. If you walked from the North Pole to the South Pole and back again, you would travel more than 24,859 miles.

The warmest temperature ever recorded was 136 degrees in El Azizia, Libya, in 1922. The coldest place is Vostok, Antarctica, which recorded a temperature of 129 degrees below zero in 1983.

70.8 percent of Earth's surface is covered in water. 29.2 percent is land.

On Earth, we call the time between sunrise and sunset "day." Day usually lasts about twelve hours. But up here in orbit the days go by much more quickly. Astronauts on the International Space Station experience sunrise and sunset every ninety minutes! That's hardly enough time to get in a good nap!

Cadets, today you will learn about how this wonderful world came to be. You will also learn that no matter where on the earth you go, from the highest peak, to the depths of the ocean or to a space station in low orbit zooming around the globe, you are surrounded by God's greatest creation. Isn't it wonderful?

Carry on, cadets, and Godspeed!

***************END VIDEO SEGMENT***************

GALILEO: Wow, commander. Earth is probably my favorite planet.

COMMANDER: **Really?**

GALILEO: **Sure. And do you know why?**

COMMANDER: **No. Why?**

GALILEO: **It's where I keep all my stuff!**

COMMANDER: **Me, too! OK, cadets. Soon you'll be spacewalking to your activity centers. Before you go, let's make sure everyone remembers our Praise Phrase. Whenever you hear someone say the first part, you respond with "Praise God!" Got it?**

GALILEO: **Ooo ooo ooo, let me do it this time!**

COMMANDER: **Go for it, Galileo.**

GALILEO: **Our God is wonderful!**

ALL: **Praise God!**

GALILEO: **They say sound doesn't travel in space, but I sure heard that!**

COMMANDER: **So did I! I don't know about the rest of you, cadets, but I'm ready to start our first mission. So everyone pay attention. Be careful on your spacewalk, and we'll see you back here for debriefing. Cadets dismissed!**

(Dismiss cadets to "Galactic Blast.")

This smaller church made a simple backdrop from unfolded appliance boxes. They added maps and paper gauges for details, and even incorporated the Praise Phrases into the scene!

Photo: Dom Lauria

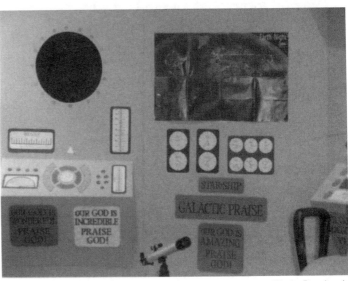

Photo: Dom Lauria

Session One Closing

(The music leader leads the children in "It's Wonderful" and "Praise God.")

COMMANDER: **Welcome back, cadets. I hear that you all accomplished your missions. Are we ready for the debriefing?**

GALILEO: **Debriefing? I sure hope I packed enough underwear!**

COMMANDER: **No, Galileo. What I mean by "debriefing" is that we talk about what we learned in today's mission. This is the time to make sure everyone understands the lessons of the day.**

GALILEO: **I learned *so* much! I learned that we get to sing songs and play games and that snacks taste much better when they're not floating around in the air—or mixed with gorilla fur.**

COMMANDER: **I'm sure they do. But what about the lesson from today's mission?**

GALILEO: **Oh, right! I learned that God created Earth and everything else in the universe as a gift to us. It's our job to take care of it.**

COMMANDER: **Good. So tell me, are you ready for me to try to clean off all that green?**

GALILEO: **No way! I like being green! We learned today that as stewards of the earth, we should think of ways to be more green each day. You can't get more green than me!**

COMMANDER: **You sure can't.**

GALILEO: **So, being the expert on being green, I thought I could give everyone a green idea after our missions.**

COMMANDER: **That's a great idea.**

GALILEO: **Again, smartest gorilla in astronaut school. Anyway, because the first thing God created was light, today's green idea is about conserving, or saving, light. We should turn off lights we're not using, and we should switch our light bulbs to ones that use less energy, like this one.** *(Galileo points to an energy-efficient light bulb.)* **But remember to get an adult's help when changing the light bulb.**

COMMANDER: **Those are great green ideas, Galileo. I'm so glad God made this planet just for us. Our God is wonderful!**

GALILEO: **Praise God! Ha! You thought I'd forgotten, didn't you?**

COMMANDER: **I'm glad you remembered. Cadets, I'm proud of you, too. You got off to a great start today. I can't wait to start our next mission. Before we go, let's thank God for watching over us today.**

(Praying) **Dear God, thank you for the gift of the earth and every living thing on it. Watch over us and bring us all back safely tomorrow. We pray in your name. Amen.**

Cadets dismissed!

Session Two Opening

(The music leader leads the children in "It's Wonderful" and "Galactic Blast." Make announcements before the skit begins.)

COMMANDER: **Welcome back, cadets. I hope you're ready for your next mission, because we've got a lot planned for you! Did you remember to turn off the lights when you left your rooms this morning? That was Galileo's green message for us.** *(Looks around)* **Has anyone seen our green gorilla friend? I hope Galileo isn't getting into trouble.**

(A clattering sound comes from offstage.)

GALILEO: *(Offstage)* **Ow! Oh wow, hot! Hot! Hot!** *(Galileo appears.)* **Whooo! That smarts! I don't see how all those other animals that got sent into space did it!**

COMMANDER: **Did what? What did you do?**

GALILEO: **In astronaut school, we learned that animals used to be sent up in orbit in satellites.**

COMMANDER: **That's right. Dogs, cats, mice, spiders, monkeys, and chimps have all been sent into space.**

GALILEO: **Uh-huh. And since I'm in space now, I figured I'd better get to it.**

COMMANDER: **Get to what?**

GALILEO: **I sat on a light! Or your desk lamp, anyway.** *(To the children)* **Don't do that, cadets. It may sound cool, but it's hot! Really hot!**

COMMANDER: **No, Galileo. When we say "satellite"—S-A-T-E-L-L-I-T-E—we don't mean "sat on a light." We mean something that stays close by. There are human-made satellites like the Hubble Telescope, and there are natural satellites like the moon. That's one of the things we're going to talk about today.**

Did any of you see the moon last night? Was it big and bright or was it just a sliver? *(Let children respond.)*

You know, the moon is Earth's only natural satellite. It's always near us, even if we can't see it. The same can be said about God. God is with us always. Sometimes it may be harder to see or feel the presence of God, but that doesn't mean it isn't there. Today we're going to learn a little more about both the moon and the presence of God.

GALILEO: **Presents! I love presents!**

COMMANDER: **Not "presents" like gifts, Galileo. That's P-R-E-S-E-N-T-S. This kind of "presence" is P-R-E-S-E-N-C-E, and it has to do with being close by. Though when you think about it, God's presence is like a present, isn't it?**

GALILEO: **Ow. Now you've made my head hurt.**

COMMANDER: **Maybe you'll understand after our mission briefing. That means we'll need to wake up the VBS GPS.**

GALILEO: **Then you need to tell us the Praise Phrase for today, commander.**

COMMANDER: **The Praise Phrase for today is "Our God is incredible! Praise God!" Got that? So when you hear someone say, "Our God is incredible!" you yell "Praise God!" Let's try it. Galileo will lead that half of the room and I'll lead this half. Start us off, Galileo.**

GALILEO: **Let them hear you back home, everybody. Ready?** *(With children)* **Our God is incredible!**

COMMANDER: *(With children)* **Praise God!**

COMMANDER: **OK, let's turn on the VBS GPS and use our Praise Phrase to wake it up.** *(The snoring sound wave appears.)*

GALILEO: **Here we go!** *(With children)* **Our God is incredible!**

COMMANDER: *(With children)* **Praise God!**

***************BEGIN VIDEO SEGMENT**************

COMPUTER: **Hmmm? Whuh? Oh!** *(Yawns)* **Hello, cadets. I'm glad to see that your last mission was a success. Today's mission takes us to a still, small place high above the surface of the earth.**

The moon—Earth's only natural satellite. It has no air and no water, but a lot of dust. It orbits the earth 250,000 miles away. If your parents tried to drive there on vacation, it would take 130 days!

On July 11, 1969, the Apollo 11 mission was the first in which humans landed on the moon's surface. They collected samples of rocks and dust and brought them back to Earth.

The moon itself does not produce light. What we see is the sun's light reflecting off the moon's surface.

Because the moon spins at about the same speed as it orbits Earth, we're always looking at the same side of the moon. It just looks different because of what we call "moon phases." Where the earth is in relationship to the sun determines how much of the moon we can see. Even though we can't always see it, the moon is always there, just like God is always there for us.

***************END VIDEO SEGMENT***************

COMMANDER: **VBS GPS, can you show us where today's Bible lesson takes place?**

***************BEGIN VIDEO SEGMENT**************

COMPUTER: **Elijah discovered God's nearness during his time in the wilderness near Mt. Horeb. Mt. Horeb is also said to be tho place where God gave Moses the Ten Commandments and where the events that take place in the book of Deuteronomy occurred.**

Today's mission is to consider the relationship between the earth and the moon and how it is similar to the relationship you have with God. The Creator is with us, even when it seems like we're all alone.

All this moon talk is making me sleepy. Good luck, cadets, and Godspeed.

***************END VIDEO SEGMENT***************

COMMANDER: **There you have it, cadets. Your mission is to learn about how the moon stays by the earth, even when we can't see it. Think about how that relates to God's presence in our lives.**

GALILEO: **Commander? The VBS GPS left out some stuff about the moon that I already knew.**

COMMANDER: **Really? Like what?**

GALILEO: **Well, the moon is made of green cheese. And when the moon is full, you should stay inside because you might turn into a weregorilla.**

COMMANDER: **Weregorilla?**

GALILEO: **Here, gorilla! HA HA HA HA HA!**

COMMANDER: **OK, you got me.**

GALILEO: *(Gesturing toward children)* **There, cadets! HA HA HA!** *(Gesturing toward the commander)* **There, commander! HA HA HA!**

COMMANDER: **OK, cadets. You have your mission. We'll meet back here for debriefing.** *(Galileo opens his mouth but is quickly interrupted.)* **Cadets dismissed!**

Session Two Closing

(The music leader leads the children in "You and Me Together" and "Revolution.")

COMMANDER: **It is good to see you all back safe and sound and ready for your debriefing—**

GALILEO: **Ssshhh!**

COMMANDER: *(Quietly)* **What is it, Galileo?**

GALILEO: **I'm listening for the still small voice of God, just like Elijah did.**

COMMANDER: **Well, Galileo, listening is a good way to open your mind and heart to God's presence. Elijah learned that, didn't he, cadets?**

GALILEO: **I learned that sometimes you have to listen very closely so you can understand what is being said, not just by God, but also by parents, teachers, and commanders. I won't be sitting on any more desk lamps, that's for sure! I also learned that our God is incredible!**

COMMANDER: **Praise God! Good job, Galileo! Do you have a green idea for us today?**

GALILEO: **I do! Cadets, think about ways you can reuse things. If you've got a toy you've outgrown, see if there is someone else who might like to have it. Sharing things we no longer want or need is a great way to make our resources last longer.**

COMMANDER: **Cadets, you've all done well today. Before we dismiss, let's bow our heads and thank God for watching over us.**

(Praying) **Dear God, thank you for being near us and guiding us even when we can't see you. Help us listen for that still small voice that reminds us of your love. Amen.**

Until next time . . . Cadets dismissed!

(Dismiss cadets to "Galactic Blast.")

Another

smaller test church used paneling as a backdrop and incorporated individual lights and light rope into their starship. Note the use of computer screens into the display.

Photo: Lima Jo Simon

Session Three Opening

(The music leader leads the children in "Revolution" and "Praise God." Make any announcements before the opening skit begins.)

COMMANDER: **Cadets! I'm glad to see you all made it back today. The starship Galactic Praise can get a little quiet at night with just Galileo and me here. He just wants to watch monkey movies. I'm always happy to see you, cadets, because that means another exciting day of space missions and learning about God's greatest creation!**

GALILEO: *(From offstage)* **Wait! Don't start! Wait for me! I was just looking for a pen.** *(Galileo enters, out of breath.)* **Whew! Did I miss them? Are they here?**

COMMANDER: **What are you talking about, Galileo?**

GALILEO: *(Looking around)* **Oh, man, don't tell me I missed them! I was so looking forward to meeting them!**

COMMANDER: **Meeting who?**

GALILEO: **The stars! You said we were going to see some stars today! I want to get some autographs!**

COMMANDER: **What? Autographs? No—**

GALILEO: **King Kong, Mighty Joe Young, Cheeta, Bonzo—**

COMMANDER: **No, Galileo, I was talking about—**

GALILEO: **—Clyde, Lancelot Link, Grape Ape, Magilla Gorilla—**

COMMANDER: **Galileo!**

GALILEO: **—J. Fred Muggs, Mr. Teeny—**

COMMANDER: ***Galileo!* I meant that we were going to learn about the stars out in space, not movie stars.**

GALILEO: **I guess that does make more sense, now that I think about it. Where did the stars come from, commander?**

COMMANDER: **The Bible tells us that God created every star, placed it in the sky, and gave each one a name.**

GALILEO: **Wow. How many stars are out there?**

COMMANDER: **Billions and billions, Galileo. Just in our galaxy alone there are 100 billion stars. Who knows how many galaxies there are?**

GALILEO: **God, right?**

COMMANDER: **That's right. And every star in every galaxy has a name. The Bible tells us that God has the same kind of relationship with us. The Creator knows your name, too. God knows us just like God knows the stars in the sky. Isn't that amazing?**

GALILEO: **It sure is. God can remember the names of all the stars *and* all the people?**

COMMANDER: **Yup! You know who else is good at remembering things? The VBS GPS. Cadets, are you ready to learn about today's mission? Then we need to find out today's Praise Phrase.**

GALILEO: **Oh, no, something else I have to remember!**

COMMANDER: **Come on, Galileo. If you can remember the names of all those ape actors, you can remember the Praise Phrase. Cadets, today when you hear "Our God is amazing!" what do you shout?**

GALILEO: *(With children)* **Praise God!**

COMMANDER: **OK, let's try it.** *(Turn on the VBS GPS's sleep mode.)* **My half of the room will start and Galileo will lead the other half. Remember to yell really loudly to wake up the VBS GPS. Ready?** *(With children)* **Our God is amazing!**

GALILEO: *(With children)* **Praise God!**

***************BEGIN VIDEO SEGMENT***************

COMPUTER: *(Startled awake)* **Huh! Ow! Oh! You startled me, commander. Ow! I'm seeing stars.**

Greetings, cadets! It's a good thing I'm seeing stars, because that's what we're going to learn about today. In our galaxy alone it is estimated that there are more than 100 billion stars!

Stars are giant balls of exploding gas held together by gravity. They produce light and heat in enormous amounts. On any given night, you might see as many as 2,000 stars in the sky. They come in a variety of shapes, colors, and sizes, from supergiants as big as an entire solar system, to tiny stars about a quarter of the size of our sun.

Our sun is a relatively young, medium-sized yellow star. Because it's so close to the earth, the light it gives off outshines all the other stars, which is why you can't see other stars during the day.

Remember that I said our galaxy has 100 billion stars? The universe contains more than 100 billion galaxies! The Bible tells us that God put them all in place and gave every one of them a name. That's more names than even I can remember!

***************END VIDEO SEGMENT***************

COMMANDER: **VBS GPS, what about today's Bible story?**

***************BEGIN VIDEO SEGMENT***************

COMPUTER: **We're going to learn about how God knows each of us as well as God knows the stars in the sky. We will explore Sychar, a town in Samaria, and learn how Jesus met a woman at Jacob's well. He showed her that even though they just met for the first time, God knew her even before she was born.**

Today, cadets, consider the personal relationship you have with God and understand that God knows each of you. To our Creator, you are very special. Good luck and Godspeed!

***************END VIDEO SEGMENT***************

COMMANDER: **There you have it, cadets! It's another important mission, so pay attention, be careful, and we'll see you here afterwards for debriefing.**

GALILEO: **And if you see any stars, get me an autograph!**

COMMANDER: **Cadets dismissed!**

(Dismiss cadets to "Galactic Blast.")

Session Three Closing

(The music leader leads the children in "A-M-A-Z-I-N-G" and "New Life in Me.")

COMMANDER: **Welcome back, cadets. I hope you had a good mission today. I know I learned a lot. How about you, Galileo?**

GALILEO: **Sure! I learned that I may not be famous like some ape movie star, but God knows who I am! God knows everything about us and is always with us, even when it feels like we're alone.**

COMMANDER: **Like at night when it's just you and me on the starship and everything is quiet? It's really you, me, and God, right? Our God is amazing!**

GALILEO: **Praise God! Praising God is so much fun. You know what else is fun, cadets? Being green!**

Because we talked about water in our Bible story, today's green idea is about conserving water. Turn off the water when you're brushing your teeth, and take shorter showers instead of long ones.

COMMANDER: **Thanks, Galileo. It's time for the cadets to go and for us to get back to our duties on the starship Galactic Praise.**

GALILEO: **Right! Hey, I've got an idea. Let's pop some popcorn and watch *Planet of the Apes!***

COMMANDER: **Again?**

GALILEO: **I've also got *Tarzan* and *Curious George*.**

COMMANDER: **Cadets, it looks like it's going to be another monkey movie marathon around here. Let's take a moment before you go to thank God.**

(The music leader leads the children in "Fill Me With Praises.")

(Praying) **Dear God, as we orbit the earth among the stars you hung in the sky, we are humble and thankful for your watchful eye. We are also grateful that, despite how huge the universe is, you know us, each and every one. In your name we pray. Amen.**

Cadets dismissed!

(Dismiss cadets to "Galactic Blast.")

Photo: Staff

This unfolded appliance box decorated with a radar image was the perfect way to hide a lectern!

Session Four Opening

(The music leader leads the children in "It's Wonderful" and "You and Me Together." Make announcements before the skit begins.)

COMMANDER: **Hello, cadets! I trust everyone had a good night's rest and is ready to begin our next mission here on the starship Galactic Praise.** *(Yawns)* **I'm a little sleepy today. Galileo wanted to stay up and look at stars last night. Then that silly gorilla wanted to make pictures of the stars with glue and glitter.** *(Holds up a picture of a star)* **Here's mine.** *(Holds up a picture of messy clumps of glue and glitter that looks like a big mess)* **Aaaaand here's Galileo's. We spent the rest of the night cleaning glue and glitter out of his fur.**

(Galileo enters, covered in glitter.)

GALILEO: **Boy! Was that a fun night or what!**

COMMANDER: **I was just telling the cadets what an awful mess you made.**

GALILEO: **No way! I was shiny! I was sparkly! I was glowing!**

COMMANDER: **You were covered in glue and glitter!**

GALILEO: **And it was magnificent! Didn't you like the way I swung through the halls like a comet?**

COMMANDER: **Trailing bits of glue and glitter on the walls and ceiling—**

GALILEO: **Exactly! It was** *so cool.* *(To the children)* **You should have been here.**

COMMANDER: **I guess it depends on where you're standing. Actually, cadets, Galileo has a good point.**

GALILEO: **Finally!** *(Pause)* **Er, what is it?**

COMMANDER: **What I saw as a big mess to clean up, our gorilla friend saw as something beautiful and fun. That's what we call "perspective," and we can use perspective to show how we become shiny and beautiful when we get closer to God.**

GALILEO: **Nice, commander. Way to bring us back around to the mission!**

COMMANDER: **That's my job, Galileo, to keep us focused on what's important: our relationship with God. Cadets, what say we wake up the old VBS GPS and learn about today's mission?** *(Turns on computer)*

GALILEO: **Then we'll need today's Praise Phrase, commander.**

COMMANDER: **We sure will. We'll use your escapades last night for inspiration. Today's Praise Phrase is "Our God is magnificent! Praise God!"**

GALILEO: **Not "Our God is shiny?"**

COMMANDER: **I think we'll go with "magnificent." Are you ready to try it, cadets? My side of the room will start and Galileo's side will finish, OK?** *(With children)* **Our God is magnificent!**

GALILEO: *(With children)* **Praise God!**

***************BEGIN VIDEO SEGMENT**************

COMPUTER: **Huh? Oh! Hello, cadets! We are past the halfway mark now and—***(A comet whizzes by on the screen.)* **Whoa! That was close!**

Like I was saying, cadets, we are more than halfway through our time on the starship Galactic Praise and— *(Another comet zooms by.)* **Wow! Did you see that? Space can be a dangerous place with all the stuff flying around out here. Today's mission deals with one of the more beautiful objects in the sky.**

These are comets! Aren't they pretty? Well, they can be. Most of the time

they're just balls of dirt and ice orbiting our sun the same way the planets in our solar system do, only much faster. Comets are one of the fastest moving objects in space, zooming around the solar system at 100,000 miles per hour.

As a comet moves farther away, it freezes to temperatures of -400 degrees. But when it gets closer to the sun, it begins to melt. The dirt and dust fly off and trail behind the comet. As the sun's light reflects off the dirt particles, we see a bright fiery trail. This is the comet's tail, and it can stretch a hundred million miles!

Like planets, comets follow a regular orbit, so we know when certain comets will pass close enough for us to view. A comet is usually named after the astronomer who first discovered it. Some comets come around every few years, but others like Halley's comet can take much longer. It is due to visit us again in 2062. The Hale-Bopp comet was last seen in 1997 and won't be back for 4,000 years.

Cadets, your mission is to consider the changes in a comet as it passes close to the sun. It changes from a frozen ball of dust and dirt into something beautiful and magnificent. So too does your life change when you move closer to God. You become beautiful in the eyes of our Creator.

***************END VIDEO SEGMENT***************

GALILEO: **That's just what you were saying, commander!**

COMMANDER: **VBS GPS, where does our Bible story take place today?**

***************BEGIN VIDEO SEGMENT***************

COMPUTER: **Jericho, one of the oldest cities in the Bible, sits in what is now Palestine. It is situated on the northern bank of the Dead Sea and was built around a natural spring, making it a very important place for desert travelers. It was outside Jericho that Jesus encountered a blind beggar named Bartimaeus and performed a miracle!**

Seek out the Son of God, cadets, and you too will see the light. Godspeed!

***************END VIDEO SEGMENT***************

COMMANDER: **There you have it, cadets. Today we're going to learn about one of the miracles performed by Jesus outside of Jericho. We're also going to consider how our relationship with God changes us and makes us shine in God's reflected glory.**

GALILEO: **God can make you shiny?**

COMMANDER: **Well, yes. Sort of. I'm sure you'll understand once you've completed the mission. Be careful out there, cadets, and we'll see you back here for debriefing.**

(Dismissed cadets to "Galactic Blast.")

Session Four Closing

(The music leader leads the children in "A New Life in Me" and "God of Wonders.")

COMMANDER: **Welcome back, cadets. I'm glad to see you all made it back safely. Wasn't that story about how Jesus cured the blind man incredible? Because he was persistent, had faith, and—**

GALILEO: **—and was really loud!**

COMMANDER: **I was going to say, because he didn't listen to the people who told him to stay quiet, he received a blessing from Jesus. We can all receive God's blessing if we're willing to ask for it.**

GALILEO: **You know, commander, I believe this experience has really started to change me.**

COMMANDER: **Oh, you mean besides turning you green and covering you with glitter?**

GALILEO: **Sure. I can feel myself growing closer to God each day.**

COMMANDER: **That's wonderful, Galileo. I can see the change as well. Our God is magnificent!**

GALILEO: **Praise God! Ha! You're not going to sneak one past me.**

COMMANDER: **I guess not. Do you have a green message for us?**

GALILEO: **Sure. Cadets, remember when I talked about leaping around the station pretending to be a comet? I made a pretty big mess, but we cleaned it up. Today's green idea is about litter. Don't toss your banana peels on the ground, and if you see someone else's trash, pick it up. We only get one planet, right?**

COMMANDER: **That's right. Cadets, you've done a great job today. We've got just one more mission left. Let's take a moment to thank the Creator.**

(Praying) **Dear God, thank you once again for your reflected glory. We are beginning to understand that as we move closer to you, we will become like a bright, shining comet, full of energy and light. Thank you for watching over us. We pray in your name. Amen.**

Cadets dismissed!

Photo: Meaghan Porter

ALL the details on this console from one larger test church are made by recycling or reusing existing materials. Very cool, and very green! Note the video game seat on the left side of the photo.

Session Five Opening

(The music leader leads the children in "A-M-A-Z-I-N-G" and "Let Everything That Has Breath." Make announcements before the skit.)

COMMANDER: *(Wrapped in space blanket with gold side facing in)* **Hi, cadets! Are you ready for today's final mission aboard the starship Galactic Praise? Good!**

You might be wondering why I'm wrapped in this space blanket. You see, I've been trying to teach Galileo about supernovas. Where is that green gorilla?

GALILEO: *(Offstage)* **It's a bird!**

COMMANDER: *(Confused)* **What?**

GALILEO: *(Offstage)* **It's a plane!**

COMMANDER: *(To the children)* **Did you hear that? There are no birds and planes in space. . .**

GALILEO: *(Bursts in)* **IT'S SUUUUPEERR NOOOOOVAAAAA! Faster than a speeding asteroid! More powerful than a black hole! Able to leap entire galaxies in a single—**

COMMANDER: **No, Galileo. A supernova isn't a superhero.**

GALILEO: **But you're wearing a cape.**

COMMANDER: *(Sighs)* **Look. I'll go through it again. Pay attention. Cadets, you watch closely.** *(Commander squats down and wraps up in the blanket with the gold side in)*. **A supernova is a kind of explosion that happens near the end of a star's life. First, the star gets very small.** *(Commander curls into a ball)* **Then it bursts into a massive display as parts of it fly across space, lighting up the sky!** *(Commander springs up and unfurls the blanket, revealing the gold side, and shakes the blanket to simulate an explosion.)* **Those parts form new stars that begin the process over again.**

GALILEO: **Ooooh.** *(Pause)* **Nope. I don't get it.**

COMMANDER: **What don't you understand?**

GALILEO: **What's your secret identity? Every superhero needs a secret identity.**

COMMANDER: **Galileo, I don't have a secret identity.** *(Takes off blanket)* **A supernova isn't a superhero. It's a star out in space. Just like us, stars grow older over time. When it gets old enough, it saves up all its energy and releases it at once, lighting up the sky and creating new stars.**

GALILEO: **Wait, so supernovas are how new stars are born?**

COMMANDER: **Born and born again, Galileo. It's a cycle that repeats itself. In some ways, it's like how Jesus died and came back to life. A star spends its life drawing things toward it. Gravity pulls in all kinds of material. The heat and light of the star change that material, and when the star explodes, everything that was drawn to it during its lifetime gets sent back out into space to form new stars.**

GALILEO: **Like Jesus drew people to him during his life!**

COMMANDER: **That's right. When he died and came back to life, he sent his message around the world, creating new followers.**

GALILEO: **Like me!**

COMMANDER: **Like you. Like me. And like the cadets.** *(Noticing the children)* **Oh! The mission! Right. We nearly forgot about today's mission.**

GALILEO: **We should wake up the VBS GPS.**

COMMANDER: **And what do we need to do that?**

GALILEO: **A secret identity!**

COMMANDER: **Galileo. . .**

GALILEO: **Kidding! I kid! We need today's Praise Phrase!**

COMMANDER: **That's right. Cadets, our Praise Phrase for the day is "Our God is awesome! Praise God!"**

GALILEO: **That should be easy to remember. You know, because God is awesome.**

COMMANDER: **Praise God! Tried to sneak one past us, didn't you?**

GALILEO: **Heh. Yeah.**

COMMANDER: *(Turns on computer)* **Well, since you're so anxious to get started, why don't you and your side of the room start us off.**

GALILEO: **Okay, cadets. Let's go.** *(With children)* **Our God is awesome!**

COMMANDER: *(With children)* **Praise God!**

***************BEGIN VIDEO SEGMENT***************

COMPUTER: *(BOOM!)* **Wow! I'm awake!** *(BOOM!)* **I'm awake!** *(BOOM!)* **Hold on!**

There. Whew! Sorry, I was gathering information about supernovas.

A red giant star has a lot of gravity pulling things toward it. Even the outer layers of the star get drawn toward the center. The energy released in the nuclear furnace at the center of the star pushes matter out.

At the end of a star's life, the star collapses in on itself. When the outer shell hits the core, the shockwave causes a huge explosion, sending pieces of the star outward at an amazing rate. The gasses and atoms form a cloud called a nebula, one of the most beautiful things to see in space.

Some supernovas are so bright they outshine the galaxy they're in. In 1054, Chinese astronomers saw a star so bright that it could be seen during the day! What they saw was a supernova, and it formed what we see today as the Crab Nebula.

Cadets, consider the cycle of life, death, and rebirth the supernova represents and how it relates to the life, death, and rebirth of Jesus. Also consider that as the pieces of that supernova shine brightly in the sky and spread material for thousands of miles in all directions, you too can be a bright shining star for God.

***************END VIDEO SEGMENT***************

COMMANDER: **That's a good point. Can you tell us about where our Bible story takes place today?**

***************BEGIN VIDEO SEGMENT***************

COMPUTER: **Well, back on Earth, of course. The road to Emmaus is near what is modern day Jerusalem. It was here that, three days after his death, Jesus spoke with some of his disciples after rising from his tomb. Today you will hear about what was said and the mission Jesus gave his people.**

Good luck, cadets, and Godspeed!

***************END VIDEO SEGMENT***************

GALILEO: **Commander, I think I understand a little more about supernovas now. But I still have a question.**

COMMANDER: **OK.**

GALILEO: **Why were you wearing the cape?**

COMMANDER: *(Ignoring the question)* **Cadets, today is your final mission. Be careful out there, and we'll see you back here for debriefing.**

Session Five Closing

(The music leader leads the children in "Praise God" and "Galactic Blast.")

COMMANDER: **Welcome back, cadets. I trust you all had successful missions.**

GALILEO: **I did! I learned that I have a mission that goes beyond our time on the starship Galactic Praise.**

COMMANDER: **You did?**

GALILEO: **Sure. Just like when a supernova explodes and sends particles around the galaxy, forming new stars, Jesus sent his disciples into the world to spread the message of his love and the love of God.**

COMMANDER: **Our God is awesome!**

GALILEO: *(With children)* **Praise God!**

COMMANDER: **Galileo, I think you've really learned something this week. Now you can share it with everyone back on Earth. You know, it says in Philippians 2:15 to "shine like the stars in the world."**

GALILEO: **I've become very shiny this week!**

COMMANDER: **You sure have. Do you have a final green idea for us?**

GALILEO: **I suggest everyone paint themselves green. Oh sure, it takes some getting used to—**

COMMANDER: **Galileo!**

GALILEO: **Kidding! I kid, cadets. Today's green idea is to recycle. Like the supernova recycles matter to make new stars, like Jesus recycles his love through each of us, you can recycle paper, plastic, aluminum, and glass to make new things and reduce the amount of trash in the world.**

COMMANDER: **That's great advice. In fact, I have something for our cadets to recycle when they get back to Earth.** *(Pass out the Outreach Seed Cards.)* **Cadets, give this card to a friend or family member who did not travel on our missions with us. When they recycle the card by planting it in the ground, flowers will grow! The flowers remind us that we should always grow in our faith.**

Cadets, I'm proud of you. You've done great work this week—but it doesn't have to end here. You've learned about space and the love of God. You've met some good friends and one silly gorilla.

GALILEO: **Hey!**

COMMANDER: **Now it is time for you to go back to Earth and make use of what you've learned here. Shine like the stars in the world. Before you go, let's bow our heads and thank our Maker for this incredible week.**

(The music leader leads the children in "Fill Me With Praises.")

(Praying) **Dear God, thank you for watching over us this week. Help us continue to grow in our understanding of the universe and our relationship with you. Help us also shine in the reflected glow of your love and be a light to those who do not know you. In your name we pray. Amen.**

Cadets, it's been a glorious week. Galileo and I hope you've enjoyed it. Until we meet again back on Earth. . . Cadets—

GALILEO: **Dismissed! Ha! I always wanted to do that!**

(Dismiss cadets to "Galactic Blast.")

Closing Celebration

The closing celebration is a program designed to tell parents, grandparents, and other family and friends what the children did at GALACTIC BLAST. The celebration combines music, puppet skits, video segments, and reading parts to describe your cadets' cosmic adventures.

Open the celebration with a church cookout. Make craft projects and discovery activities available for your guests. Then close the celebration with this program.

The program is designed to take place on the starship Galactic Praise in the assembly area, where the children have been meeting each day for opening and closing assemblies.

There are reading parts for thirty-three children. Most of the parts are only a few sentences, so children should be able to memorize their lines without too much trouble. (You can modify these parts to fit what your children experienced at GALACTIC BLAST.) The program also features the commander of the starship Galactic Praise, Galileo the Gorilla, and two appearances by the VBS GPS.

When indicated, show VBS GPS video segments from Sessions One and Five. (Use only the video segments that talk about the space component, not the sections about where the Bible story takes place.) The VBS GPS dialogue has been added to this script so it is clear what segments to use.

The order of the music for the closing celebration is as follows:
★ "Galactic Blast"
★ "Praise God"
★ "It's Wonderful"
★ "Revolution"
★ "God of Wonders"
★ "Fill Me With Praises"
★ "You and Me Together"
★ "A-M-A-Z-I-N-G"
★ "A New Life in Me"
★ "Let Everything That Has Breath"

Photo: Matt Huesmann

Closing Celebration

COMMANDER: **Hello, everyone! It's time to start our galactic celebration!**

(The children enter singing "Galactic Blast." Alternatively, have the children in position and ready to sing before the program begins.)

COMMANDER: **Welcome to our starship Galactic Praise, where we've had a super cosmic adventure praising God! As our theme song says, "we got a mission, a lifetime plan... Give God the glory for all we see."**

We want to show you everything we did at GALACTIC BLAST. We learned about outer space, experienced God's love, and met new friends. In fact, we should introduce you to another member of our crew. Joining us on our missions was Galileo the Gorilla—the latest member in a long line of animal astronauts and, as Galileo likes to say, the smartest gorilla in astronaut school.

We learned that gorillas are very shy creatures, so to make Galileo feel welcome we have to make our best gorilla noises. Can we do that again?

(Everyone makes gorilla sounds.)

GALILEO: *(Springs in quickly)* **Who's there?** *(Sees everyone and reacts as if frightened)* **Aaagh!** *(Recovers)* **Wow! Look at everybody!**

COMMANDER: **Galileo, these new people are the friends and family of our cadets.** *(Looks at Galileo)* **Um, don't you think it would be a good idea if you let them know why you are green?**

GALILEO: **Oh, you mean, tell them about the accident in the cafeteria?**

COMMANDER: **Yes, that's what I mean.**

GALILEO: **Well, I was looking around for a good place to build a nest. We gorillas like a comfy bed of leaves and grass to sleep on. Anyway, I thought it made sense to sleep near the food, so I went to the cafeteria. As I was looking around I saw this big, red, shiny button—the one that says "Do Not Push"—and I decided to push it.**

COMMANDER: *(To the audience)* **That particular button controls the gravity in the cafeteria!**

GALILEO: **Yeah, and the next thing I knew, I was floating around the room through clouds of food. There was guacamole, lime Jell-o, key lime pie, green Kool-Aid, broccoli, bell peppers, green beans, olives—**

COMMANDER: **And you and the green food became one.**

GALILEO: **Yes! But after all I learned at GALACTIC BLAST, I understand how cool it is to be "green," so I decided to stay green.**

COMMANDER: **Our first mission got us all thinking about the importance of being "green." In that mission, we learned all about creation. We had some help from our VBS GPS—our Galactic Praise Satellite. Let's view again what the VBS GPS told us on our first mission.**

GALILEO: **OK, but first we have to wake up the VBS GPS. . . and you know what that means.**

COMMANDER: **We need to shout our Praise Phrase, and I know a fun way to do it. Let's sing "Praise God." That has *all* of the Praise Phrases in it.**

(The children sing "Praise God." As the song ends, begin the video segment from Session One.)

COMPUTER: *(Springing to life)* **Shngnhg . . . huh?! What? Oh! Hello, commander! The VBS GPS is ready with your mission briefing on the creation of the universe. We'll be focusing on your home planet, Earth.**

Let's see . . . Earth . . . Earth . . . There it is! Earth is the third planet from the sun.

The Earth is over 24,901 miles around its widest point. We call this the equator. If you walked from the North Pole to the South Pole and back again, you would travel more than 24,859 miles.

The warmest temperature ever recorded was 136 degrees in El Azizia, Lybia, in 1922. The coldest place is Vostok, Antarctica, which recorded a temperature of 129 degrees below zero in 1983.

70.8 percent of Earth's surface is covered in water. 29.2 percent is land.

On Earth, we call the time between sunrise and sunset "day." Day usually lasts about twelve hours. But up here in orbit the days go by much more quickly. Astronauts on the International Space Station experience sunrise and sunset every ninety minutes! That's hardly enough time to get in a good nap!

Cadets, today you will learn about how this wonderful world came to be. You will also learn that no matter where on the Earth you go, from the highest peak, to the depths of the ocean or to a space station in low orbit zooming around the globe, you are surrounded by God's greatest creation. Isn't it wonderful?

Carry on, cadets, and Godspeed!

***************END VIDEO SEGMENT***************

COMMANDER: **It *is* wonderful! Hey, cadets, let's tell everyone how wonderful it is!**

(The children sing "It's Wonderful." As the song ends, speakers 1 and 2 come to the microphone.)

COMMANDER: **During each mission these cadets learned a Bible story, a Bible Booster memory verse, a space connection, and a Praise Phrase. We'll tell you about each of our missions.**

CHILD #1: **Our first mission was the creation of the universe. We learned how "in the beginning" there was nothing but God. Then God spent the next six days creating everything!**

CHILD #2: **Our space connection told us about our planet Earth. God carefully placed everything in space and on the earth so it all works perfectly.**

COMMANDER: **The motion of the universe is perfect. Everything spins around and around, never stopping. In the same way, God's love always orbits each one of us.**

(The children sing "Revolution." As the song ends, speakers 3 and 4 come to the microphone.)

CHILD #3: **We learned a Bible Booster verse with each mission. Our first Bible Booster is from Psalm 24:1: "The earth is the LORD's and all that is in it, the world, and those who live in it."**

CHILD #4: **The first mission's Praise Phrase is "Our God is wonderful!"**

ALL: **Praise God!**

(The children sing "God of Wonders." As the song ends, speakers 5–8 come to the microphone.)

CHILD #5: **Our second mission was to Mt. Horeb. We met Elijah at the top of the mountain. He was hiding in a cave.**

CHILD #6: **Elijah was running away. God came to the mountain to speak to Elijah. Elijah experienced a strong wind, an earthquake, and a roaring fire. But God was not in the wind, earthquake, or fire. God spoke to Elijah in a still small voice.**

CHILD #7: **Our space connection on the second mission taught us about the moon. We learned that the moon never leaves Earth's side. Even when we can't see the moon, it is always near Earth.**

CHILD #8: **We must remember that God never leaves us. God is always near us, hearing our prayers and ready to help us.**

COMMANDER: **Prayer is such an important way for us to talk with God. We learned to use prayer time as a time to ask for help but also as a time to give thanks and praise to God.**

(The children sing "Fill Me With Praises." As the song ends, speakers 9 and 10 come to the microphone.)

CHILD #9: **The Bible Booster is Psalm 73:28a: "But for me it is good to be near God."**

CHILD #10: **The second mission's Praise Phrase is "Our God is incredible!"**

ALL: **Praise God!**

(The children sing "You and Me Together." As the song ends, speakers 11–16 come to the microphone.)

CHILD #11: **Our third mission took us to Samaria, where Jesus stopped by a well for a drink of water. He met a woman at the well and spoke to her. Jesus knew all about her, even though she did not know him.**

CHILD #12: **The woman was amazed at all that Jesus knew. When she learned that he was God's Son, she praised him by bringing others to him to learn more about him.**

CHILD #13: **The space connection taught us that God created all of the stars and put each one of them in place.**

CHILD #14: **God gave all the stars a name, and God knows each of them. God knows each one of us, too.**

CHILD #15: **Our Bible Booster is Psalm 139:1: "O LORD, you have searched me and known me."**

CHILD #16: **The third mission's Praise Phrase is "Our God is amazing!"**

ALL: **Praise God!**

(The children sing "A-M-A-Z-I-N-G." As the song ends, speakers 17–26 come to the microphone.)

CHILD #17: **Our fourth mission took us to just outside the city of Jericho. Jesus met a blind beggar sitting along the road.**

CHILD #18: **The blind beggar called out to Jesus and asked that Jesus show mercy on him. The townspeople wanted the beggar to be quiet.**

CHILD #19: **Jesus asked that the blind beggar be brought to him. He gave the blind beggar his sight.**

CHILD #20: **He told the beggar that his faith made him well. The beggar followed Jesus, praising God for all that had happened.**

CHILD #21: **In the space connection, we learned about comets. A comet is a ball of ice crystals and dust that flies through space.**

CHILD #22: **When this dirty snowball gets close to the sun, the ice begins to melt and the pieces of dirt reflect the glow of the sun.**

CHILD #23: **Because of the solar wind around the sun, the dirt particles break apart and a tail is formed.**

CHILD #24: **The comet helps us remember that when we grow closer to Jesus, we are changed. We begin to reflect the light of Jesus.**

CHILD #25: **Our Bible Booster verse is Psalm 29:4: "The voice of the LORD is powerful; the voice of the LORD is full of majesty."**

CHILD #26: **The Praise Phrase for the fourth mission is "Our God is magnificent!"**

ALL: **Praise God!**

(The children sing "A New Life in Me." As the song ends, speakers 27–33 come to the microphone.)

CHILD #27: **In our fifth mission we met two disciples walking on the road between Jerusalem and Emmaus. They had been in Jerusalem for the Passover celebration.**

CHILD #28: **While in Jerusalem they learned about Jesus' death on a cross. They knew Jesus had been buried in a tomb but learned that morning that the tomb was empty.**

CHILD #29: **A stranger joined them on their walk. They told the stranger all that had happened. When they reached their home in Emmaus, the two disciples invited the stranger into their home for a meal.**

CHILD #30: **As the stranger blessed the bread they were about to eat, the two disciples realized the stranger was Jesus. Jesus vanished! The two disciples returned to Jerusalem, praising God and telling others what had happened. Jesus is alive!**

CHILD #31: **Our Bible Booster is Psalm 18:46: "The LORD lives! Praise be to my Rock! Exalted be God my Savior!"**

CHILD #32: **The space connection for this mission taught us about a supernova. A supernova is a giant star that eventually explodes, creating many new stars. Our VBS GPS can explain it best.**

CHILD #33: **To wake up VBS GPS let's say our final Praise Phrase. "Our God is awesome!"**

ALL: **Praise God!**

COMPUTER: *(BOOM!)* **Wow! I'm awake!** *(BOOM!)* **I'm awake!** *(BOOM!)* **Hold on!**

There. Whew! Sorry, I was gathering information about supernovas.

A red giant star has a lot of gravity pulling things toward it. Even the outer layers of the star get drawn toward the center. The energy released in the nuclear furnace at the center of the star pushes matter out.

At the end of a star's life, the star collapses in on itself. When the outer shell hits the core, the shockwave causes a huge explosion, sending pieces of the star outward at an amazing rate. The gasses and atoms form a cloud called a nebula, one of the most beautiful things to see in space.

Some supernovas are so bright they outshine the galaxy they're in. In 1054, Chinese astronomers saw a star so bright that it could be seen during the day! What they saw was a supernova, and it formed what we see today as the Crab Nebula.

Cadets, consider the cycle of life, death, and rebirth the supernova represents and how it relates to the life, death, and rebirth of Jesus. Also consider that as the pieces of that supernova shine brightly in the sky and spread material for thousands of miles in all directions, you too can be a bright shining star for God.

****************END VIDEO SEGMENT***************

Godspeed, cadets!

COMMANDER: **Yes, we can all be bright and shining stars for Jesus. This cosmic adventure has drawn us closer to God. After learning about creation and all of the wonderful, amazing, and awesome things God has done, we have learned to love God and praise God so much more than before.**

To close our celebration, we want to sing a final praise song. This song is our Galactic Praise Bible Booster, Psalm 150:6: "Let everything that breathes praise the LORD!" Please join the children as we praise the Lord.

(The children lead the audience in "Let Everything That Has Breath.")

Photo: Meaghan Porter

Closing Traditional Worship Service

Call to Worship

The earth is the Lord's and all that is in it, the world, and those who live in it. Let us come and worship the Lord God Almighty.

Music

"God of Wonders"

Opening Prayer

Dear God, we come to worship you, to give you praise, and to thank you for all that we have and are in this world. Be with us as we gather for this time of worship. Open our hearts, our minds, and our ears to hear your word this morning. We pray this in Jesus' name. Amen.

Music Selections

"You and Me Together"
"It's Wonderful"

Proclamation

LEADER: **God is our creator; the maker of the universe and all that is in it.**
PEOPLE: **Our God is wonderful! Praise God!**
LEADER: **God is always near us; ready to help us, guide us, and comfort us.**
PEOPLE: **Our God is incredible! Praise God!**
LEADER: **God knows us all by name, just as God knows each star in the heavens.**
PEOPLE: **Our God is amazing! Praise God!**
LEADER: **The voice of the Lord is powerful; the voice of the Lord is full of majesty.**
PEOPLE: **Our God is magnificent! Praise God!**
LEADER: **The Lord lives! Praise be to God, our Savior.**
PEOPLE: **Our God is awesome! Praise God!**

Music

"Praise God"

Scripture

John 4:28-30, 39-42
Luke 18:42-43
Luke 24:31-35

Music

"A-M-A-Z-I-N-G"

Message (Sermon Topic)

A Celebration Praising God

Offering

Music

"A New Life in Me"

Sending Forth

Go forth into this new week praising God with a thankful heart, praising God in recognition of all that God has made, and praising God for the new life given to each of us.

Music

"Let Everything That Has Breath"

Closing Contemporary Worship Service

Welcome

**The earth is the Lord's and all that is in it,
the world, and those who live in it.
Let us come and worship the Lord God Almighty.**

Music

"God of Wonders"
"Let Everything That Has Breath"

Offering

"Revolution"

Scripture

John 4:28-30, 39-42
Luke 18:42-43
Luke 24:31-35

Message (Sermon Topic)

A Celebration Praising God

Song of Response

"A New Life in Me"

Closing

"It's Wonderful"